D1710275

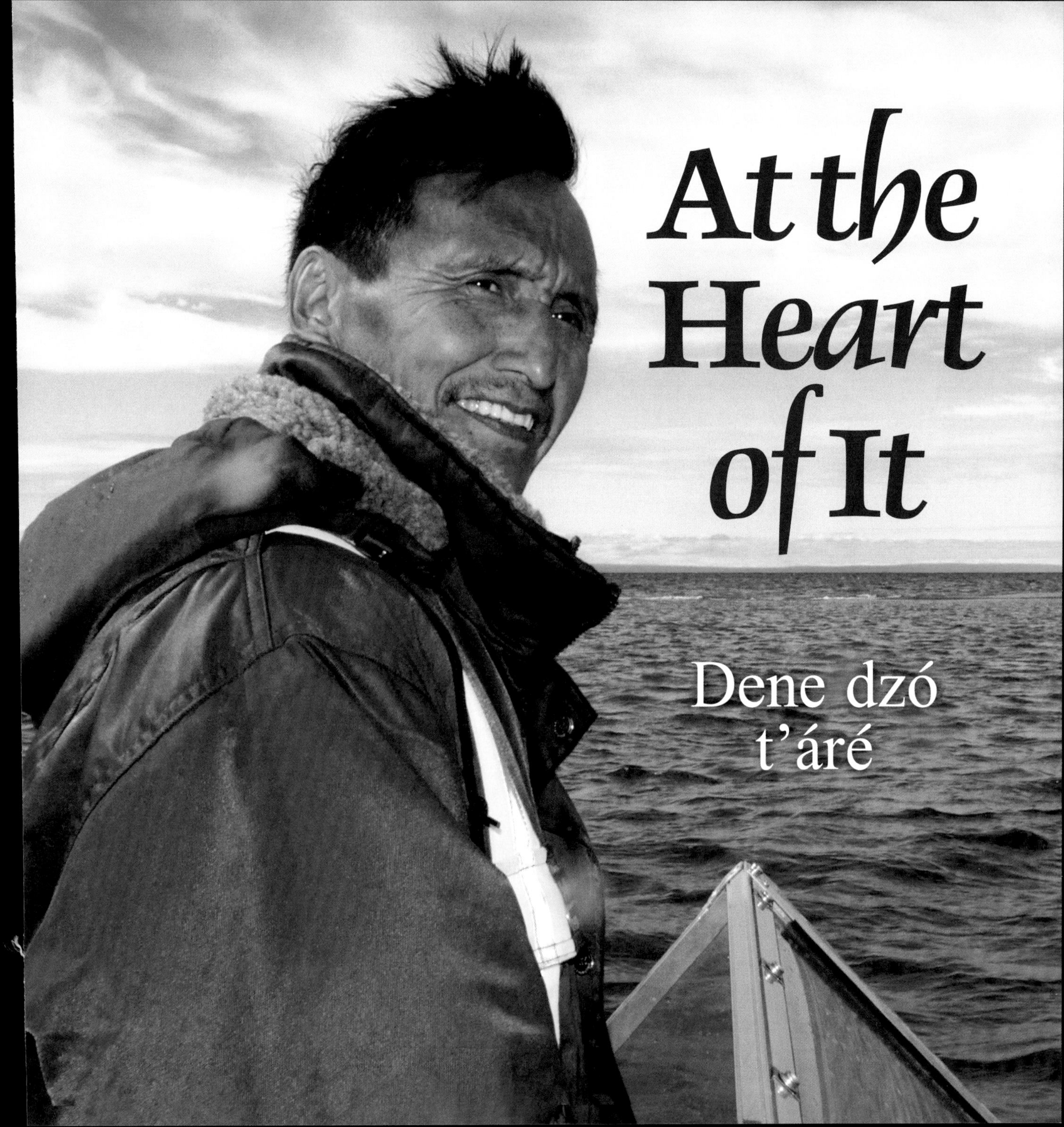

At the Heart of It

Dene dzó t'áré

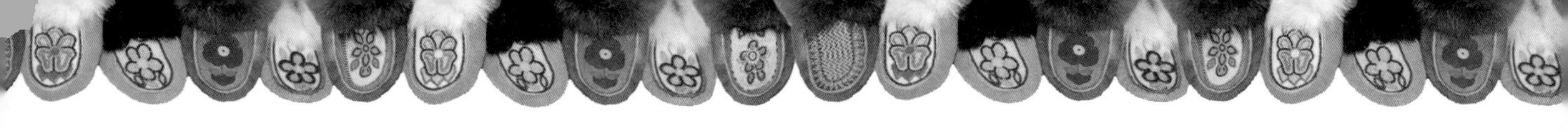

Fifth House Ltd.
A Fitzhenry & Whiteside Company
195 Allstate Parkway
Markham, Ontario L3R 4T8
1-800-387-9776
www.fifthhousepublishers.ca

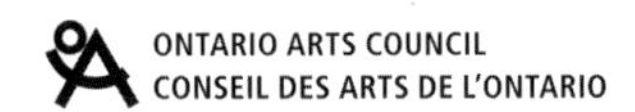

First published in the
United States in 2012 by
Fifth House Ltd.
A Fitzhenry & Whiteside Company
311 Washington Street
Brighton, Massachusetts,
02135

Cover and interior design by John Luckhurst
Photography by Tessa Macintosh
Additional illustrations and photographs by: Dot van Vliet, Prince of Wales Northern Heritage Centre (PWNHC) (map, page vi); Morris Neyelle (hockey, page 5); Library and Archives Canada (George Back painting, page 5); Susan Irving, PWNHC (artifacts, page 5); Fran Hurcomb PWNHC (Bear Rock, page 6); Alasdair Veitch (mountains, page 6); Richard Fennie/NWT Archives/N-1979-063-0143 (trucks, page 7); Rene Fumoleau (George Kodakin, page 8); PWNHC, unknown photographer (Ayha, page 8); Paul Vecsei (moon over lake, page 10); Wayne Lynch (geese over moon, page 11); Paul Vecsei (trout, page 20); Dene Nation (logo, page 25); GNWT Department of Education (map, page 25).
Series editorial by Meaghan Craven

The type in this book is set in 10-on-15-point Trebuchet Regular and 10-on-13-point Tekton Oblique.

Fifth House Ltd. acknowledges with thanks The Canada Council for the Arts and Ontario Arts Council for their support of our publishing program. We also acknowledge the financial support of the Government of Canada through the Canada Book Fund.

The author would like to thank The Canada Council for the Arts for generously funding the writing of this book. She would also like to thank The Nature Conservancy, Canadian North Airlines, The Sahtú Board of Education, Denendeh Investments Incorporated, and Shehtah Nabors for financial assistance in the completion of this book.

Printed in Canada by Friesens on Forest Stewardship Council (FSC) Approved paper

2011 / 1

Library and Archives Canada Cataloguing in Publication

Willett, Mindy, 1968-
At the heart of it = Dene dzó t'áré / Mindy Willett, Raymond Taniton, Tessa Macintosh.
(The land is our storybook)
Text in English and Sahtugot'ine.

ISBN 978-1-897252-69-7

1. Drum-Construction. 2. Tinne Indians-Music. I. Taniton, Raymond II. Macintosh, Tessa, 1952- III. Title. IV. Title: Dene dzó t'áré.
V. Series: Land is our storybook

ML1035.W45 2011 786.9'1923089972 C2011-905590-2

The Sahtú region is known for its incredibly talented artists, especially the makers of moose- and caribou-tanned moccasins decorated with beautiful beadwork and trimmed with fur. Raymond's parents, Alfred and Jane, show their moccasins made by Jane.

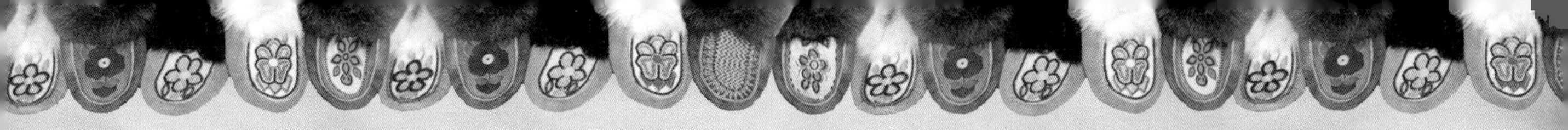

Acknowledgements

We are indebted to Raymond's parents, Alfred and Jane Taniton, who raised their children to be true Dene. Your strength of character and how you shared your knowledge with us is a true testament to what you believe in. To Bernadette and all your children, Martyann Kenny, Leanna, Mary, Miles, Leela, Nicholas, and especially Hailey (who worked so hard to translate for her grandparents and was truly listening and learning): we could see your desire to know more. Thanks to Raymond's brother, Gary, who was a huge help around the camp, and to Raymond's grandsons, Isaiah and Caleb, and nieces, Brittney Kenny and Angel Mackeinzo, who were patient listeners and wonderful models for the photographs. We truly hope you remember the stories and are able to pass them on. A huge *Mahsi* also goes to Raymond's daughter, Leanne, who helped translate for her grandparents, and sister, Edith, who did the written translations.

So many other community members gave us guidance. We are indebted to Chief Raymond Tutcho and the other councilors of the Délı̨ne First Nation, especially Morris Neyelle and Charlie Neyelle, who shared their knowledge openly. We are grateful to the Kodakin family. During the Spiritual Gathering, the entire community made Mindy and Tessa feel welcome. Délı̨ne is truly a magical place.

To Erica Hughes and her grade 5 students at ʔehts̀éo Ayha School in Délı̨ne, especially Shawn Baptiste, Arabella Elton, Faith Gaudet, Jordan Ford, John Roche, Tyler Smith, and Joy Vital. Your help with the editing was greatly appreciated.

We are grateful to our friend Dot van Vliet for designing the map and to the rest of the staff at the Prince of Wales Northern Heritage Centre for their assistance. Thanks to Paul Vecsei, who generously shared his incredible photos of Great Bear Lake. Thank you Erica Janes of the Canadian Parks and Wilderness Society, John Stewart of the Department of Education, and Karen Hamre of the Protected Areas Strategy for reviewing the manuscript. Thank you, Margaret Bertulli and Henry Cary of Parks Canada for sharing their exciting excavation with us. Thanks to Darrell Beaulieu, Seamus Quigg, Mike Palmer, Richard Jeo, Charlotte Hoffmann, and Pete Ewins for making the book possible. And thank you Meaghan Craven, John Luckhurst, and Stephanie Stewart of Fifth House Publishers for going the extra mile in every way.

Tessa would also like to give many thanks to her very supportive brother, Malcolm, and equally enthusiastic sisters, Alexandra and Sara. Though far away, they are always near and dear to her heart.

Mindy is thankful for her husband Damian Panayi who takes care of their two beautiful children, Jack and Rae, while she's away researching these books. Thanks for editing, listening, and being my best friend.

Raymond would like to personally thank Bernadette and their children for all their knowledge and support.

Mahsi.

To all Sahtugot'ine.
Let us work together
to keep our culture and
history alive and to
remember who we are
as Dene people.

At the Heart of It

Dene dzó t'áré

By RAYMOND TANITON
and MINDY WILLETT
Photographs by
Tessa Macintosh

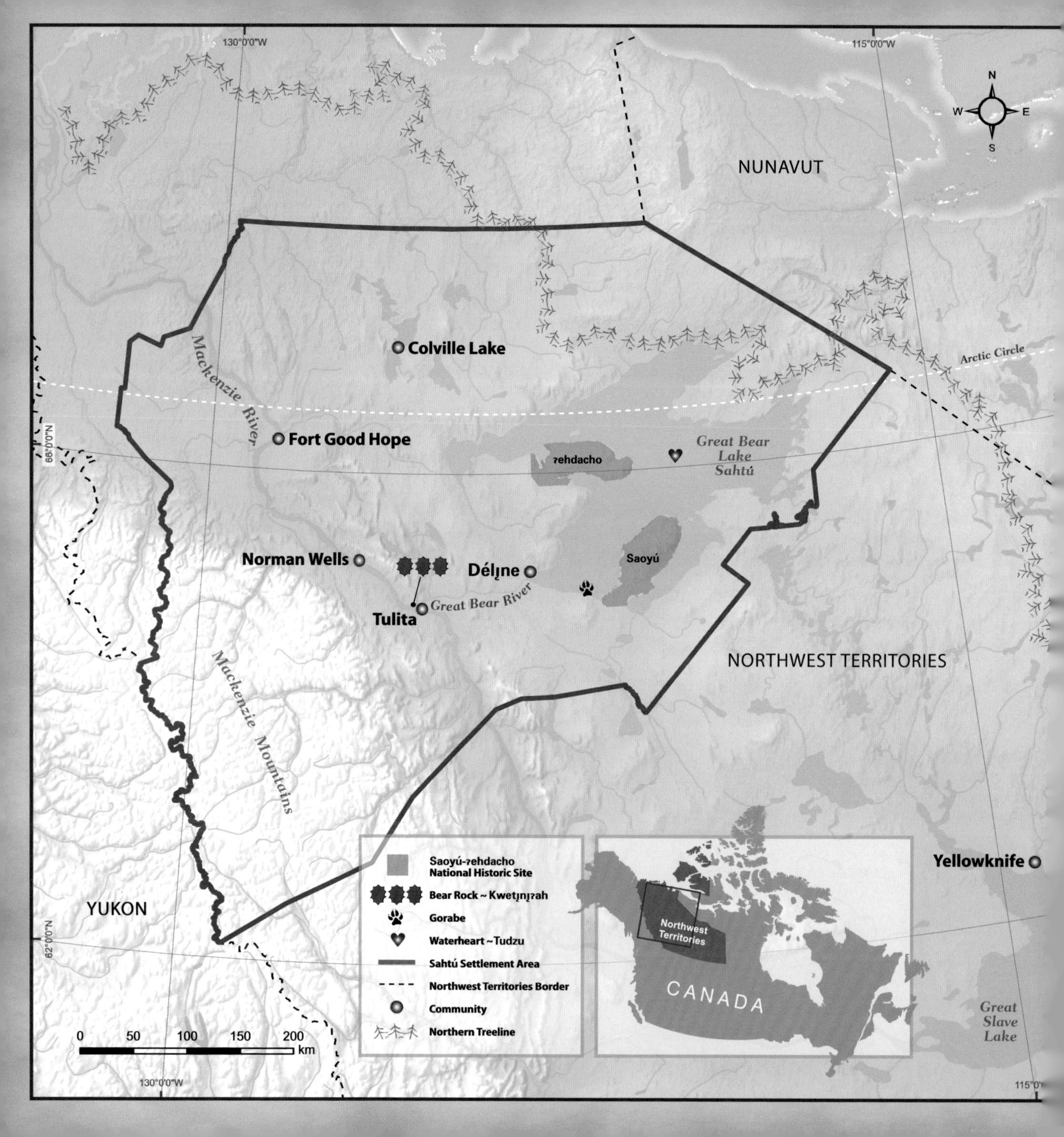
130°0'0"W
115°0'0"W
N
W
E
S
NUNAVUT
Arctic Circle
Colville Lake
Mackenzie River
Fort Good Hope
66°0'0"N
ʔehdacho
Great Bear Lake Sahtú
Norman Wells
Délı̨ne
Saoyú
Tulita
Great Bear River
NORTHWEST TERRITORIES
Mackenzie Mountains
Saoyú-ʔehdacho National Historic Site
Bear Rock ~ Kwetı̨nı̨ʔah
Gorabe
Waterheart ~ Tudzu
Sahtú Settlement Area
Northwest Territories Border
Community
Northern Treeline
Northwest Territories
CANADA
Yellowknife
YUKON
62°0'0"N
0 50 100 150 200 km
Great Slave Lake
130°0'0"W
115°0'

Séhłéé,

I am Raymond, son of Alfred and Jane Taniton, grandson of Louie and Rosia Taniton and Jean and Camilla Karkeye. I am proud to be Sahtugot'ine, which means "the people of Great Bear Lake." I live in Délı̨ne, on the shore of this great lake that we call Sahtú. When people come here they are impressed with our respectful youth and beautiful community. They ask me to describe what we do here to make it this way.

After England colonized Canada, Aboriginal peoples were made to do things differently, forget their traditional ways and values, and become different people Sahtugot'ine also suffered from colonialism, but we continued to teach our children our core values: to have respect for their Elders, their parents, and themselves.

I tell people there are many reasons why we are a strong and healthy community. But one thing is for certain. We have never given up our responsibility to govern and look after ourselves. **We** are responsible for our healthy families and our connected community. **We** are responsible for ensuring our youth know who they are as Dene people and for keeping our land and water clean. **We** elect strong and gifted leaders, but each of us is responsible for his or her life choices. For us, **responsibility** is at the heart of it.

Mahsi Cho,

Raymond Taniton

Raymond Taniton

Meet My Family

I have been married to Bernadette Taniton for 31 years. When we met, women looked for hardworking husbands. Men, too, we looked for women who got up early in the morning to work and were good sewers and cooks. Of course, we also wanted spouses who knew how to laugh and love.

Together, Bernadette and I have 5 daughters, 2 sons, 6 grandchildren, and a large extended family. No marriage is perfect. I have made mistakes, but we try to learn from our mistakes and listen to each other to work out our problems. We get guidance from Elders, and from our parents and grandparents.

Raymond's family in front of his home, which he built with help from a friend in 1987.

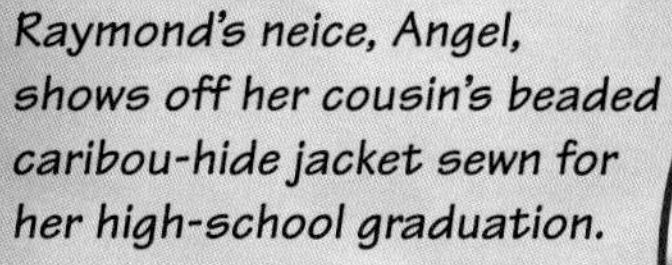

Raymond's neice, Angel, shows off her cousin's beaded caribou-hide jacket sewn for her high-school graduation.

Bernadette makes incredible bannock to share with her family and community.

Raymond's parents, Alfred and Jane Taniton, are both respected Elders in the community.

Bernadette and her niece, Brittney, pick blueberries together. They will add the berries to bannock and pies or make jam.

A strong healthy family is at the heart of it.

About 600 people live Déline ("where the river flows"), which is just a few kilometres from the mouth of Sahtú *De* (Bear River) on the shore of Great Bear Lake. Our ancestors used this area to support our traditional way of life: hunting, fishing, and gathering.

In Déline we take care of one another. If a hunter gets a moose, caribou, or some fish he will share it with those who need it most. Déline became a permanent settlement when the Canadian government built a school here in 1952. At that time our community became known as Fort Franklin, because the explorer Sir John Franklin spent the winters here in 1825, 1826, and 1827. Franklin selected the area because it is an excellent fishing place and could provide food for him and his 50 men.

When I was chief in our community in the 1990s, we worked to change the name of our community back to Déline. We felt our town name should be in our language and reflect our culture.

A connected community is at the heart of it.

The tipi-shaped building, where Raymond and fellow band councilor Morris Neyelle are meeting, is an example of how modern buildings reflect traditions.

Many youth in Déline speak their Aboriginal language.

Most yards in Délı̨ne have tipis in which people prepare meat.

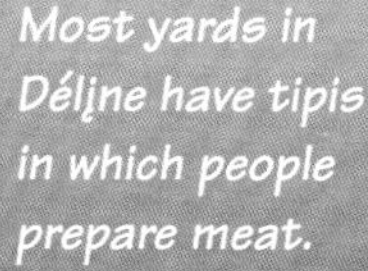

Fort Franklin History

The earliest recorded use of the word "hockey" in Canada is in a letter Franklin wrote in 1825: "We endeavour to keep ourselves in good humour, health, and spirits by an agreeable variety of useful occupation and amusement. Till the snow fell the game of hockey played on the ice was the morning's sport..."

Raymond and other community members work with Parks Canada staff to protect the national historic site where Franklin overwintered. Archaeologists from the Prince of Wales Northern Heritage Centre have unearthed the remains of a stone chimney and other artifacts like this button, arrowhead, and awl.

Winter view of Fort Franklin, *a watercolour by George Back, who journeyed with Franklin in 1825–27.*

Sahtú Region

Délı̨ne is one of five communities in the Sahtú Region. Norman Wells is the regional centre. It is also called Tłegǫ́hłı̨, "where there is oil." The Dene have always known where to get oil and used it to waterproof canoes. When Canadian government leaders learned about it in 1920, they decided to make a treaty here to gain control of the oil. This area became part of Treaty 11. Decades later, we wanted to have more control of our land than Treaty 11 allowed.

The five Sahtú communities worked together to achieve a land claim. Deciding to sign a land claim was hard. Some people worried that we were giving too much of our land and rights away to the federal government. The leaders who worked on the claim didn't decide for the people, though. We gave the people all the information we had, and in the end 90 per cent of the Sahtú Dene and Métis people voted in favour of our land claim.

The Sahtú is geographically diverse. Norman Wells is located in the southwest part of the Sahtú and has mountain views. The northeast part is tundra and the taiga dominates central areas.

Raymond was chief of Délı̨ne during the negotiation of the land claim. His style of leadership is that of a tough negotiator.

The beautiful Our Lady of Good Hope Roman Catholic Church is in Fort Good Hope. It is a National Historic Site.

During World War II the US government wanted to move fuel from Norman Wells to military bases in Alaska. They built roads and pipelines through Dene traditional lands without permission. The project was called the CANOL (Canadian Oil) Pipeline Project and operated for less than a year. With a signed land claim, projects like a pipeline won't happen again without the Dene being part of the decision.

Bear Rock is near the town of Tulita, where the Mackenzie and Bear rivers meet (see the map at the beginning of the book). It is where the Dene cultural leader, Yamoria, killed the giant beavers that were making trouble for the people. The Dene Nation logo tells this story. Yamoria put their pelts up on the rock. Can you see the pelts on the mountain and in the logo?

Our Leaders

Strong and gifted leaders have always been the key to Dene people's survival. We value many different kinds of leaders, including cultural, political, spiritual, and hunting leaders. Traditionally a leader is someone who is a really good hunter or is mystically tied to a particular animal or place. Good leaders take advice and direction from the Elders. Leaders know that important decisions should not be made quickly by one person but after much discussion and as a group. A leader must have an open heart and open mind. He or she must be able to listen to people.

Mount Clark (Beh Deo) is visible from Délı̨ne. When the world was new, Yamoria sat on this mountain and made the dip in its peak. He pushed the rocks with his feet trying to find the giant beavers that were causing problems for the people.

In Délı̨ne we value the prophecies given to us the prophets Ayha, *Joseph Bayha, Joe Naedzo, and "Old Andre." Our leaders make decisions based on the prophecies they gave us. ?ehtseo Ayha lived according to the old ways. Many of his predictions came true. When he was young no Christian priest had yet come to Délı̨ne. Ayha had a vision in which a voice told him about God. Even though he could not read, he was somehow able to read all the stories in the Bible when a priest arrived in Délı̨ne. Many people travelled great distances to see the prophet Ayha and to pray with him.*

George Kodakin *was chief for 10 years in the 1970s and 80s. He was part of the Dene Nation and led the people through difficult times when we were forced to change from traditional to modern ways. At that time we were caught between two worlds. People really listened when he spoke. He never mixed up his words or had to pause to search for the right words. He always spoke the truth from his heart and touched a lot of people. He had knowledge and wisdom.*

Ethel Blondin Andrew *is a Mountain Dene from Tulita and was the first Aboriginal woman to be elected to the Canadian Parliament. She represented the NWT in Ottawa with the Liberal Party from 1988–2006, winning 4 elections in a row. Before becoming a politician, she was one of the first Aboriginal teachers in the North. She continues to work hard to help all people, especially youth and women, and to promote the North's cultures.*

Today our chief is Raymond Tutcho. *He's a family man and a good hunter. He goes out on the land all the time. He always tries to make things better for the people. Like all past chiefs, he works together with the members of the council to make the best decisions for the community. He works hard for the future.*

George Blondin *was a dynamic leader. He was elected chief of Délı̨ne in 1984 and had many leadership roles with the Dene Nation. He is most remembered for his leadership in storytelling. He worried that many of the traditional stories were being lost when the old people died. He interviewed many storytellers from all over the North and wrote several books. He became a member of the Order of Canada.*

My mom, Jane Taniton, *is a cultural leader in our town. She has helped women deliver babies, is an amazing sewer, can tan any kind of hide, and is always helping others in our community. She shares her knowledge with the younger generation.*

Leanne Taniton *is my daughter. She is studying in Victoria, BC. She intends to return home and work for the Territorial Government. Leanne translates Sahtugot'ine into English. Dene roots keep her strong and grounded. She is a young leader and role model.*

Strong and gifted leaders are at the heart of it.

Our spiritual leaders help us make healthy life choices. Our choices are part of what holds us together as a community. We try to be thoughtful about what we do. In the morning we get up, cross ourselves, and say *Mahsi* because we are thankful for a new day. We look to the sun getting up, greeting us, and we are grateful. We look to the setting moon and we are grateful.

Prophet Andre is the source for all the spiritual songs we sing. He received these songs in his visions. When Prophet Andre could no longer play, he gave Johnny Neyelle his drum and Johnny became lead drummer. When it was time, Johnny passed the drum on to my dad, Alfred. My dad is now the keeper of the drum and the songs that go with it. He's getting tired, and it takes a lot of energy to be the drum leader. Soon he'll have to pass Andre's drum and songs on to someone else.

Feeding the Fire

As described by Alfred Taniton

A fire is a living thing. We offer things to, or "feed," the fire and make sure what we offer is completely burned. You can't just walk away from an offering to the fire. You need to talk to the fire, keep it going to help you live a long life. By feeding the fire we speak to our ancestors who have passed on. Whenever we kill something, such as a caribou, our ancestors' hands are all there, lifting us up, helping. And they wait to be fed. We feed the fire to honour them and give them some of our harvest. I play my drum and sing a prayer song when I feed the fire.

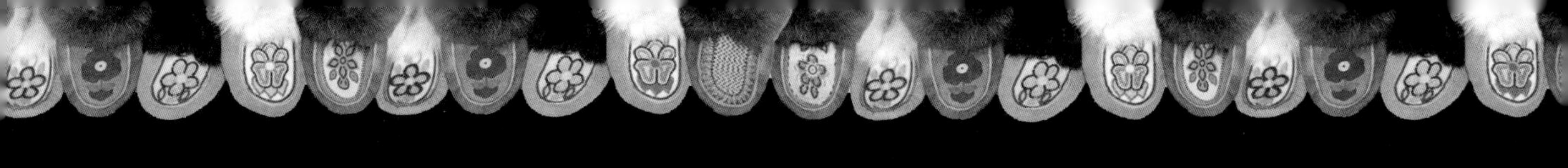

The drum is very special to us and connects us with the land and the animals. Last fall when we were drumming a flock of snow geese flew by. The flock passed over us then circled and came back. They seemed to be listening. Their voices were calling with our voices when we were singing Prophet Andre's song.

The creator gave us trees to make drums. My father is an expert drum maker. He shares his knowledge with young people.

How to Make a Drum

Instructions by Alfred Taniton, Keeper of the Drum

❶ *The best tree for a drum is a tall, straight, spruce. It should have small branches and the cones should come off easily.*

❷ *For a good-sized drum frame, plane the tree so that it is at least 100 cm long and about 1 cm thick.*

Soak the wood in hot water to make it soft. Also soak some babiche and a piece of caribou hide in hot water. (You'll need these later!) When the wood is soft, bend it into a circle and fasten the ends with wooden pegs and glue. Poke a line of holes in the frame about 5 cm apart from one another.

❸ *Attach the softened babiche to the drum frame and weave it together in the centre. The babiche gives the drum the strength it needs to stay round. Don't forget to string one piece of babiche tightly around the outside of the frame.*

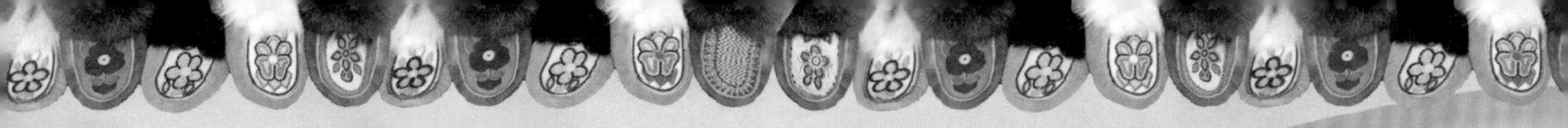

❹ Now drape the wet caribou hide over the frame and keep it in place with a string of babiche. Be careful not to touch the centre part of the skin while stretching it over the frame. If you do, fingerprints will remain on the drum.

❺ Using an awl, poke holes through the hide in the same places where you put holes in the frame. Attach the hide to the frame by stringing babiche through these holes. Start a piece of babiche inside the drum, carry it through the hole and over the babiche that encircles the frame, then push it back through another hole to the inside. Repeat until the hide is securely attached to the frame.

❻ Cut off the extra hide and babiche, then dry the drum carefully over the fire. The heat from the fire will shrink the hide so that it tightens on the frame.

❼ When the drum is dry, attach two pieces of babiche so that they run parallel down the centre of the drum. These give the drum a rich sound when you strike it with the stick. The drum is now ready to be played!

Our drum is at the heart of it.

19th Annual Spiritual Gathering

Sahtugot'ine have strong faith in our traditions, and most of us practice the Roman Catholic faith. Each summer we hold a spiritual gathering in Déline. At the gathering, Charlie Neyelle, one of our spiritual leaders, retells the story of the prophets. We also pray, reflect on our lives, and enjoy one another's company.

As the keeper of the drum, Alfred led the drummers in the drum dance and opened the 19th Annual Spiritual Gathering with a prayer song.

At the spiritual gathering, people place some food, tobacco, or another important item into a bowl. Charlie Neyelle prays, blesses the offerings, and then feeds them to the fire.

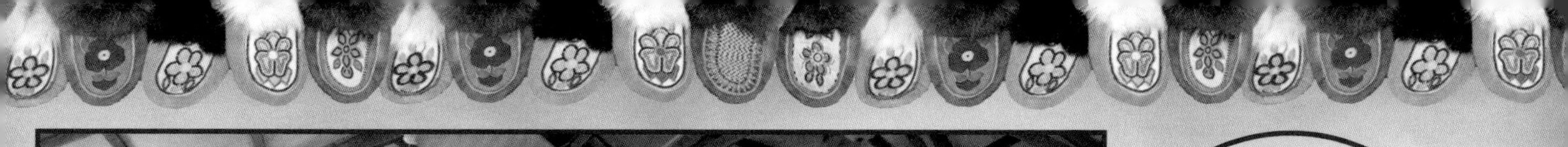

During the spiritual gathering in 2010, 23 children received First Communion. Two Franciscan friars from New York came to Délı̨ne to help welcome the young people into the Church.

In 1991 the people of Délı̨ne made one of the prophecies true by building a new log cabin on the site of Prophet Ayha's old house. It is used as a gathering place. It is here that Charlie shares stories about the prophet. On the front steps of Prophet Ayha's house, Raymond shares laughter with his father and friends.

Having faith is at the heart of it.

My father, like all our respected Elders, has many stories to share. The features of the land hold our history. Stories about the land tell us who we are as Dene people. Most of our stories come from a particular place on the land.

When you spend time with Elders during different types of activities, they may tell you stories. But the Elders won't tell their stories to just anyone. You have to be around, be patient, and listen to be rewarded with a good story like the one my grandson Isaiah experienced.

Isaiah was watching closely when my mom was cooking a big trout. My dad noticed Isaiah's interest and so found the fish bones that illustrate a story that took place long ago when the world was new. In this story, the tools needed to survive were handed out to the animals and the fish grabbed the knife, spear, axe, and harpoon.

Great Bear Lake is famous for its large and numerous fish. The fish bones story is easily illustrated with a large trout because the bones in the shape of the tools are easy to spot. Can you guess which bone is which tool?

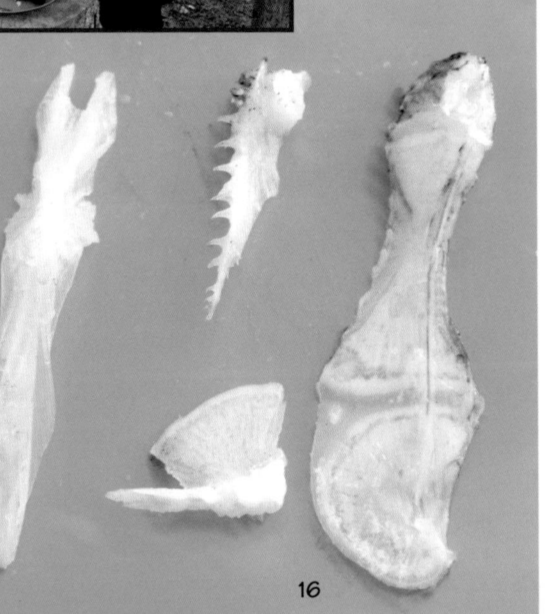

Our Words

English	*Sahtugot'ine*
song	*shį*
drum	*eghele*
fish	*łue*
storytelling	*godi*
leader	*t'akwo k'áowe*
trout	*sahba*
Elder	*Dene ʔohda*
knife	*beh*
spear	*ʔeht'į́*
axe	*gohkę*
harpoon	*la'hwhi*

Moose-hide Ball is a game I remember the Elders playing a lot when I was a kid. On long summer nights they'd play for hours under the midnight sun. It's a fun game. You don't keep score and it's not about winning or losing. To play you need a big open space and a small ball that will fit in the palm of your hand. To make the ball, you take a piece of moose or caribou hide, stuff it with wet moss,
and sew it shut.

To start the game the men would throw the ball to one another while the women tried to get it. If a woman caught the ball, she would try to hold onto it while the men tried to get it back. The game can be quite rough! Women are very strong from working so hard. When women caught the ball, it might even take two men to get it out of their hands. Everybody would be piled up on top of one another trying to get the ball. What a lot of fun we had!

Our Stories

Sahtú k'aowe (The Lake is the Boss)

Told by Alfred Taniton

A long time ago when the world was new a giant wolf lived in a cave. The cave was on an important travel route for the people, about 40 km from Délı̨ne on the south shore of Great Bear Lake. At that time people used canoes to get around. When people paddled near the cave the wolf would swallow them. He killed a lot of people, so they started portaging around the cave to avoid him. One time there was a young girl with a group of travellers. She was behind the group when she saw the wolf move out of the cave and walk into the water. The wolf was growly singing, "Gora, gora, gora." He turned around and looked at the girl. They both looked at each other, and the wolf turned to stone.

Today, when it is calm, you can clearly see the outline of a wolf when you are a little way back from the island. This island that used to be the wolf is called Gorabe because of the wolf's song. When the wolf turned to stone, it became safe to pass this island.

It is also safe to go and visit the cave now. Our Elders taught us to show respect to the power of the land by making an offering at the entrance of the cave. Some Elders have told stories about how they once dared themselves to go inside the cave so they could find out more about their futures. My father, Louie, was one of those brave ones. To see how long you will live, you must go way to the back of the cave and then run out. If you trip partway, you might have some problems in life. If you fall, you will have a short life. If you make it out without falling, you will live long. There is nothing to trip over in there, but some who've tried have fallen. It's true. My father did it, and he didn't fall. He lived to be 105.

If you pass the island in a boat you should pay the water something that is important to you. This is because there used to be a whirlpool here that would swallow canoes. To make sure you have a safe passage you should pay the water to show respect because the lake is the boss.

An offering to the lake can be anything that is important to you. Brittney chose to offer a quarter to the lake to ask for a safe journey home.

While Raymond stands on one of the wolf's ears he points to the mouth. He tells his grandson, Caleb, not to pass the island right in front of the wolf's mouth because it is guarded by unseen powers. Passing this way in the springtime can give you snow blindness.

Can you see the wolf's ears? To see all of the island go to pages 24 and 25.

Our land is alive with the stories of our people. It also feeds our people. Before he died, the great leader George Kodakin told me that we must protect our "freezer" for future generations. Our freezer is Great Bear Lake.

Délı̨ne has worked for years to protect the lake and the land around it. We were one of the first places in Canada to protect part of our land because of the stories the land holds. Saoyú–ʔehdacho National Historic Site is the largest protected national historic site in Canada. We know that our land must be conserved for our stories to stay alive.

When we say "our land" we mean much more than land. We mean the water, the air, the animals, and everything on the land. Our land is alive. The centre of all this life is what we call, Tudze or Waterheart. The story of Tudze has been passed down through many generations.

Our Stories

Tudze or Waterheart

Told by Alfred Taniton

There was a powerful medicine man called Kayé Daoyé. He was spiritually connected to the land and animals, especially a type of fish called loche, who is king of all fish. One day, after setting four hooks, he found one of them missing. This was upsetting because hooks were valuable. That night, as he dreamt, he travelled to find the fish that had taken his hook. As he

moved through the centre of Sahtú, he became aware of a great power in the lake: the heart of the lake. We call this Tudze or Waterheart. Around the heart swims a huge fish, and from this large fish all the other fish come.

The people say that Waterheart is sacred so we should leave it be. We can talk about it, but we are not allowed to search for it. Through his dream Daoye realized that all life is connected. He gave us this message: Everything in this world, everything you see is alive. The land, the water; it's all alive.

We're telling this story now and will keep telling it, but nobody should look for Waterheart. It's so powerful. It feeds everything surrounding the centre. Waterheart is working to take care of the lake and everything around it.

Sahtú k'aowe *"the lake is the boss." We are the keepers of this lake, of this Waterheart. It is so important that nothing destroys it. Someday, people from all over the world will try to come here because we have so much freshwater. We need to protect the lake.*

Our stories are at the heart of it. They help us to know who we are and where we come from.

I like to take my children and grandchildren out on our land. I feel good walking around, feeling the presence of the old people. They had a hard life, nothing like we have today, and yet they survived and were happy. We want to educate our young people about the old ways. Even if they don't live like our ancestors, they will always remember what it means to be Sahtugot'ine.

Sahtú k'aowe. *The waves on the lake can be so high that travel is not possible. People are patient and wait until the lake tells them it is safe to travel again.*

The land is our storybook. It is our school, our library, our church. It is where we learn our stories and where we discover who we are as true Dene people.

The land is at the heart of it all.

All the Details!

babiche - thread made out of hide (skin).

colonialism - when one nation dominates and controls another and makes that other nation follow its rules.

Délı̨ne (del-la-nay) - where the water flows

Denendeh - land of the people; a large portion of the Northwest Territories, excluding Inuit lands in the northern part of the territory (although Dene did use these lands in the past).

North Slavey - a group of languages and people designated by the government of Canada for the purposes of traders travelling to Fort Norman (now Tulita). Before contact, the people of this region recognized themselves as four distinct groups including: the Hare, Mountain, Willow Lake, and Bear Lake peoples. Raymond's family belongs to the Bear Lake people, or Sahtugot'ine.

séhłéé - one who is one with me; one who makes me whole; my friend.

Sahtú - a region; the lake known as Great Bear Lake in English (the largest lake solely within Canada's borders and the 7th largest lake in the world). Despite mining on its eastern shore, Sahtú is also one of the last pristine lakes of its size in the world. The Sahtú region has 5 communities including: Norman Wells, Fort Good Hope, Colville Lake, Tulita, and Délı̨ne.

Sahtugot'ine - (saw-two-go-tin-eh) the people of Sahtú (Great Bear Lake); the language spoken in Délı̨ne.

sinew - thread made out of tendons.

taiga -the forested area just south of the tundra in cold wet climates. Spruce trees are the dominant tree on the taiga.

treeline - not a specific "line" on a map, but the point at which trees—having become smaller and smaller and more and more spread out the farther north one travels—stop growing.

tundra - treeless lands.

The Dene Nation is an Aboriginal organization that represents all the Dene of the NWT. Its logo represents one of the Yamoria stories that tie the 5 Dene groups together. The logo is a large drum with the land of the people, or *Denendeh*, represented by the rivers and mountains.

Arrows - Yamoria shot two arrows into the place where Great Bear River and the Mackenzie River meet. Each spring, when the ice breaks, you can see two big poles sticking out of the river.

Beaver Pelts - These represent the three giant beavers Yamoria killed and their hides, which he stretched on Bear Rock. He made the world safe by getting rid of the animals tha were harmful to the people.

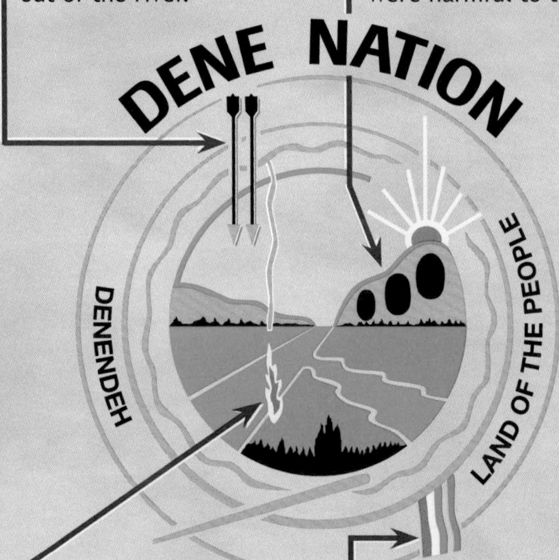

Flame - Yamoria cooked the beavers, and the beavers' fat started to burn. The fire continues to burn to this day.

Ribbons - Each of the 5 coloured ribbons represen one of the 5 Dene Nation tribes and language groups: North Slavey, South Slavey, Chipewyan, Tłı̨chǫ, and Gwich'in.

Timeline of Délı̨ne Events*

8000 BCE - Giant beavers roam the NWT. Called *Castoroides ohioensis*, they are up to 2.5 metres tall and weigh 60-100 kilograms —about the size of a black bear. Dene still tell stories of the giant beavers, which illustrate the length of time Dene have used this land called *Denendeh*.

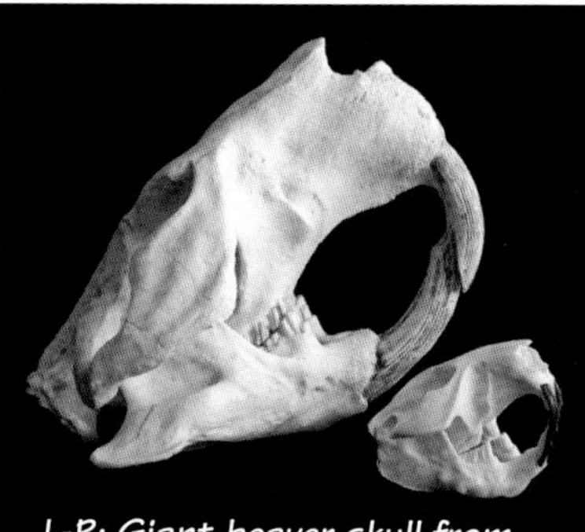
L-R: Giant beaver skull from long ago; beaver skull today.

1799 - The North West Company establishes a trading post near Délı̨ne.

1825-1827 - The Hudson's Bay Company sets up a trading post at Délı̨ne called Fort Franklin.

1921 - Spurred on by Imperial Oil, which found oil at Norman Wells in 1920, the Canadian government extends Treaty 11 to the Dene people of the area. It is signed in July in Tulita, formerly Fort Norman. Treaty 11 is the last of the Canadian numbered treaties.

1933 - Great Bear Lake's uranium is mined and then used in nuclear bombs that kill many Japanese during World War II. Many Dene men who work in the uranium mine eventually die of cancer.

1947 - Prophet Ayha dies.

1952 - Fort Franklin, a permanent community, is established in Délı̨ne.

1987 - Archaeologists from the Prince of Wales Northern Heritage Centre with assistance from the people of Délı̨ne excavate Old Fort Franklin and find artifacts like those shown on page 5.

1993 - The 5 Sahtú communities sign one land claim on September 6, 1993. Raymond Taniton is chief and signs on behalf of Délı̨ne.

2009 - Saoyú (saw-you)-ʔehdacho (eh-dah-cho) becomes a protected area. Parks Canada and Délı̨ne co-manage the protected lands.

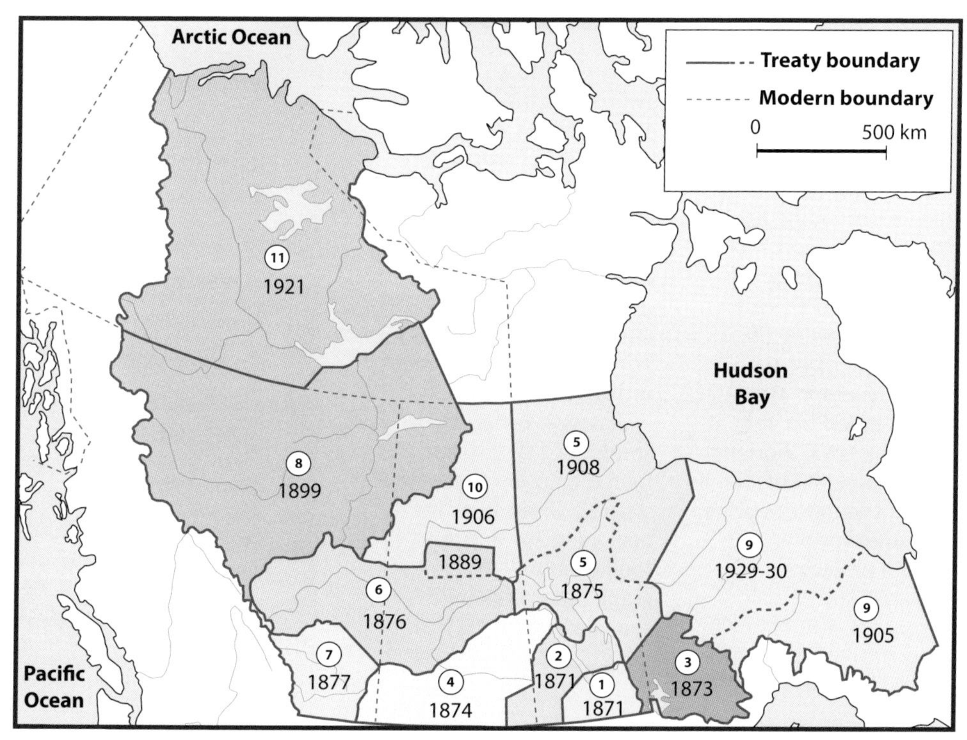

Canada's numbered treaties and the year in which the treaties were signed.

* *For details on each of the events, go to the NWT Timeline at:* www.pwnhc.ca.

About the Authors and Photographer

Raymond Taniton is Dene from Great Bear Lake. He grew up living off and learning from the land. He has worked his entire life for the betterment of his people. He was chief of Délı̨ne and grand chief of the Sahtú Dene. As a long standing and active supporter of the Protected Areas Strategy Committee, Raymond worked with others to see two peninsulas on Great Bear Lake, Saoyú–ʔehdacho, become permanently protected as a National Historic Site.

Mindy Willett is a mother, an educator, and a passionate advocate for all things northern. This is the seventh book in *The Land is Our Storybook* series she has co-authored with storytellers from the official language groups of the Northwest Territories. Growing up among the pines of the Canadian Shield in Atikokan, Ontario, helped her feel at home in the NWT. Working with Raymond and his family on one of the most pristine lakes in the world was an incredible privilege.

Tessa Macintosh is an award-winning northern photographer who raised her family in Yellowknife. In 35 years she has been fortunate to photograph many wonderful northerners and fantastic places across the North. Her photos illustrate 6 other books in *The Land is Our Storybook* series, and her work is included in *Canadian Shield* (2011). She has fond memories of previous visits to Great Bear Lake, beginning 30 years ago, toddler in tow, to photograph Elders making snowshoes.

The Land is Our Storybook

Titles in *The Land is Our Storybook* series, all co-written by Mindy Willett and illustrated by Tessa Macintosh:

We Feel Good Out Here,
by Julie-Ann André

The Delta is My Home,
by Tom McLeod

Living Stories,
by Therese Zoe and Philip Zoe

Come and Learn with Me,
by Sheyenne Jumbo

Proud to be Inuvialuit,
by James Pokiak

The Caribou Feed Our Soul,
by Pete Enzoe

At the Heart of It,
by Raymond Taniton

The first four titles in the series are also available in French!